We Pathfinder

You've taken a brave step toward your own physical, mental, and spiritual growth. May this journal serve you well as you step forward on your floatation journey.

Floatosophy: the authors created term that means the philosophy of floating. This self-guided interactive journal was created to help its readers get the most out of their float experience.

There is no path to Happiness.
Happiness is the path. There is no
path to Love. Love is the path.
There is no path to Peace. Peace is
the path.
-- Dan Millman

PREFACE

Floating will help you become a better human being. And by floating you will help make the world a better place to live. So, thank you for floating, and doing your part! This journal is designed to help you explore who you are, where you are, why you're here, and how you will uniquely incorporate the lessons learned into your daily life. This interactive journal is packed with challenges and opportunities for transformation. No Pathfinder makes it through life without the aid of tools, resources, and allies. Floatation therapy is one such tool and this guide is to be used as one of your resources. Please consider everyone in the float community your ally on this journey. Each person is unique and requires a different set of tools, so allow your wisdom to guide you, as you float, to discover other tools you may need to incorporate to help align you with your path and your desired outcomes.

The author has no formal training in mental, physical, or spiritual health, but is an experienced floater. The tips and techniques he provides throughout this guide are things that have worked for him and other floaters in the float community. There is no right way or wrong way to float, nor is there a correct way to use this manual or interpret your feelings and visions as you float. Therefore, please feel free to use this self-guided journal in any way you like. The author has organized the journal in a logical way to take you from zero to hero in floatation therapy if you decide to read it from page one to the end.

"Peace comes from within. Do not seek it without"
--Buddha

Table of Contents

The Power of Journaling.....................6-7

What is Floating..................................8

Benefits of Floating............................9-12

Floating vs Other Modalities.............13-15

Discounted & Free Floats..................16

Research & Clinical Studies..............17

Where to Float...................................18-19

Getting Ready for First Float.............20-22

Pre-Float Preparation.......................22-24

Quieting the Mind.............................25-26

Mind-Body Connection......................27-28

Spirit-Body Connection.....................29-32

Your First Float.................................33-37

After Your Float................................38-39

First Float Journal Entry...................40-41

Seven Thoughts on Floating.............42

Intentions...44-45

Reframing...46

The Power of Words..........................47

Your Second Float............................49-53

The Ouroboros.................................56-57

Decluttering the Mind.......................58-60

Trauma and Floating........................61-63

Shadow Work................................ ...64-65

Ego Death..66-69

Third Float & Beyond.......................70-73

Targeted Float Techniques...............74-79

Famous Floaters..............................80-83

Float Journals................................ ...84-93

Post 12 Float Assessment................94-95

Winning Combination........................96-97

Interactive Resources.......................98

THE POWER OF JOURNALING

Journaling is an ancient tradition, one that dates to at least 10th century Japan. To get the most of your float experience. I recommend you keep a journal; you can start by using this guide but should transition to a more formal journal after a few floats. You should document each float, how you felt before, your intention going in, what happened, and how you feel after. Not only will it help you track your progress, but evidence supports that journaling provides other unexpected benefits. The act of writing accesses your left brain, which is analytical and rational. While your left brain is occupied, your right brain is free to create, intuit and feel. In summary, journaling and floating helps remove mental blocks and allows you to use all of your brainpower to better understand yourself, others, and the world around you.

Clarify your thoughts and feelings.

Do you ever seem all jumbled up inside, unsure of what you want or feel? Taking a few minutes to jot down your thoughts and emotions (no editing!) will quickly get you in touch with your internal world.

Know yourself better.

By writing routinely you will get to know what makes you feel happy and confident. You will also become clear about situations and people who are toxic for you — important information for your emotional well-being.

Reduce stress.

Writing about anger, sadness and other painful emotions helps to release the intensity of these feelings. By doing so you will feel calmer and better able to stay in the present.

30
S M T W T F S
1 2 3
4 5 6 7 8 9 10
11 12 13 14 15 16 17
January, 2015 18 19 20 21 22 23 24
Friday 25 26 27 28 29 30 31

My 10th float...

My intention was...

Fully relaxed...

No longer stressed

Remember to

Solve problems more effectively.

Typically we problem solve from a left-brained, analytical perspective. But sometimes the answer can only be found by engaging right-brained creativity and intuition. Writing unlocks these other capabilities, and affords the opportunity for unexpected solutions to seemingly unsolvable problems.

Resolve disagreements with others.

Writing about misunderstandings rather than stewing over them will help you to understand another's point-of-view. And you just may come up with a sensible resolution to the conflict.

In addition to all of these wonderful benefits, keeping a journal allows you to track patterns, trends, improvement, and growth over time. When current circumstances appear insurmountable, you will be able to look back on previous dilemmas that you have since resolved, and it will give you the strength to continue forward.

WHAT IS FLOATING?

Floatation therapy is an escape from the constant stress of life's daily pressures and a natural way to heal the body, mind, and soul. The concept is similar to the mineral salt baths in the Dead Sea in Israel. A floatation tank contains eight hundred to one thousand pounds of Epsom salts, which are dissolved into water about 10 inches deep, and maintained at skin temperature. This environment allows your body to float on top of the water without any effort, and your body is no longer affected by earth's 9.8 pounds of gravity. This, combined with the light proof and sound proof nature of the tank or room, deprives you of your human senses bringing your body back into homeostasis.

BENEFITS OF FLOATING

Deep Relaxation. Floating with no gravity, no light, and no sound, is one of the fastest and most effective ways to elicit the body's natural relaxation response and enter a state of deep relaxation. Your brain responds by removing undesirable chemicals and releasing endorphins, stimulating feelings of happiness and well-being.

Stress Relief. Stress correlates with increased levels of cortisol, and in floatation therapy there is a natural tendency for cortisol to be reduced. For this reason, floatation therapy is one of the few noninvasive techniques available to manage stress. Daily life has a tendency to take you away from yourself. It's not uncommon for people to be in a state of constant stress activating the "fight-or-flight" response multiple times during the day. This can be brought on by any number of events such as traffic, inconsiderate people, or looming deadlines. Over time, such low-grade chronic stress can lead to high blood pressure, increased heart rate, and muscle tension. Visiting a floatation spa helps people counteract the toxic effects of chronic stress by slowing their breathing rate, relaxing their muscles, and reducing their blood pressure. People often report feeling refreshed, rejuvenated, and better able to cope with life's minor annoyances after floating.

Among the great things which are to be found among us, the being of nothingness is the greatest.
-- Leonardo da Vinci

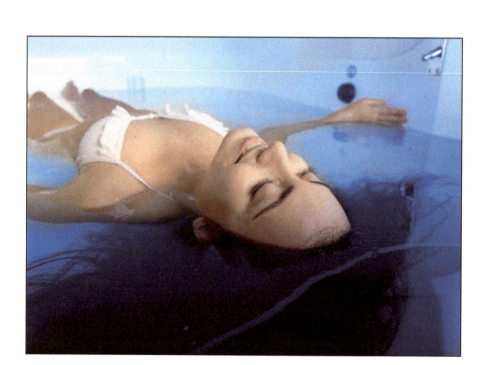

Pain Management. Research has shown that regular use of the float tank can help health problems that are caused or exacerbated by chronic stress such as fibromyalgia, insomnia, hypertension, anxiety disorders, and migraines. By invoking the relaxation response, blood flow increases to all parts and systems of the body, including the brain, creating a whole body healing effect. Floating also provides relief from the constant downward push of gravity, the single greatest cause of wear and tear to bones, joints and body tissue. The zero gravity effect also provides relief from discomfort during pregnancy.

Enhanced Creativity and Focus. Being inside the floatation tank, where sensory input is eliminated, produces a mental state where one's learning abilities are at their highest and powers of visualization and auto-suggestion are greatly enhanced. As the float progresses, there is a transition from beta or alpha brainwaves to theta which can last indefinitely throughout the float without losing consciousness. With practice one can increase the amount of time that they spend in the theta state. Many use the extended theta state as a tool for enhanced creativity and problem solving or for super learning. With the brain being held in a theta state wave-length, the mind becomes hyper-suggestible. With less distractions and greater resources at its disposal, the mind is able to absorb new material very deeply, with research showing improved performance in memory and recall activities.

Enhanced Physical Performance. Although athletes often turn to floatation therapy in order to cope with an injury, floatation therapy can actually be used to enhance athletic performance as well. Floating can help to relax muscles so that an athlete is better prepared physically for a big event, but it can also be used to enhance mental clarity in athletes. Since floatation therapy is able to impact both your mental and physical capabilities, it is an invaluable practice for serious athletes. As floating enhances your mental and physical abilities, you will experience a dramatic improvement in your overall athletic performance. The relaxation caused by floating can help to take pressure off of the tired joints and muscles that might be causing you pain. Floating also helps your whole body to relax so that your muscles align properly, thereby preventing injuries and helping speed your recovery time when you are dealing with an injury. Cross-fit athletes, MMA fighters, long distance runners, and even professional golfers have been utilizing floatation therapy for some time. Several college and professional sports teams are incorporating it into their standard practices. Whether you're a professional athlete, or play a sport for exercise or hobby, you can benefit from floating.

Floating vs Other Traditional Modalities

Self health care can be very expensive, but it is an investment worth making to bring peace, health, and happiness to your life. Traditional doctors, therapists, and chiropractors are much more expensive than alternative wellness modalities, like floating, because these practitioners are required to take years of study and get certified. Arguably not only is floating cheaper, but floating is better because it holistically targets the root of the problem vice just treating the symptoms with pharmaceuticals, which can have other undesirable side effects. So the main benefits of floatation therapy are: it is cheaper, more effective, and healthier than traditional health care.

Also, when alone by yourself in the dark, you cannot hide or lie to yourself, about what is really going on. You may have the best therapist in the world, but if their clients are not honest with them, they will not be able to effectively help. With floating, it is just you. No one is touching you, no one is judging you, no one is pushing you to do something you don't want to do. It is just you! As a result, you are sometimes your own best therapist. You won't give yourself more than you can handle and don't be too judgemental on yourself. Yes, using floating along with traditional therapy can probably accelerate some healing and help you to better understand what you are feeling. But you will eventually figure it out yourself. The mind, body, spirit connection is super powerful if we just give it time and space in a float tank. You must learn to love yourself before you can love anyone else and floating alone in the dark will force you to love yourself.

In a float tank you won't be able to tell if your eyes are open or closed. You will just be.

In addition, for some, therapy, has a negative stigma attached to it, and people don't like to admit they need help or have a problem and therefore won't seek professional help. However, floating will help them too. Some people start off floating to improve their physical performance to make them better athletes, or help them recover faster from an injury, or to help them perform better on an exam, vice thinking they need some mental health or spiritual calibration. Since floating synergizes the mind, body, and soul, all at once, floaters cannot just focus on just one aspect. They will get all three whether they want them or not. So floating helps people that don't think they need help in other areas, if they commit to getting in the float tank for other less altruistic reasons.

"If you can't love yourself, how the hell you gonna love somebody else?"

--RuPaul

DISCOUNTED AND FREE FLOATS?

The general cost of a float across the industry should be based on the average cost of a massage for the same time frame in whatever city you are located. Most float centers offer specials and discounts for first time, frequent floaters, and members, so make this a part of your discovery when visiting multiple float centers. In addition, some float centers have localized free float programs for special communities like first responders, veterans, active military and their families. Some offer specials on certain days of the week. So make sure you ask.

If you are going to have a hard time funding your floating habit, other than the float centers themselves, you can look into using your Health Savings Account (HSA) to float. Each provider is different, but in general if a doctor says it will help you, then the HSA company should cover it.   Also, asking your boss to offer it as a Corporate Wellness benefit is a "win win" for everyone. Employees are less likely to miss work, work more efficiently, be nicer, and develop new and innovative ideas when floating.

There is also a national nonprofit, called the National Float It Forward Association (NFIFA) that provides free floats to active military, veterans, first responders, and their immediate families utilizing the float centers closest to the floaters.   Visit their website, www.nfifa.org to learn more or help provide free floats to this community. Portions of the proceeds from this book will go to NFIFA to help fund these free floats.

RESEARCH AND CLINICAL STUDIES

Floatation therapy is still considered on the fringe of modern western medicine. Most traditional doctors, health insurance, and the Veteran's Administration do not recognize it as a therapeutic solution for mental health issues. However, pathfinders like Dr. Justin Feinstein, Director of the Float Clinic and Research Center (FCRC) at the Laureate Institute for Brain Research (LIBR) in Tulsa, Oklahoma is leading the way with clinical floatation research. His early studies have demonstrated that floating in the right environment can provide powerful relief for patients suffering from anxiety, post-traumatic stress disorder (PTSD), and depression. The floatation community is anxiously waiting for floating to receive the recognition it deserves. To review all the current clinical research and publications on floatation therapy please visit www.clinicalfloatation.com/publications.

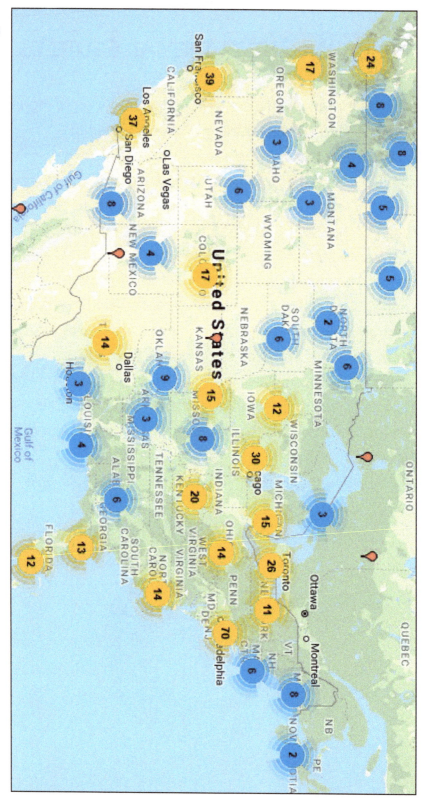

WHERE TO FLOAT?

Floatation Therapy has been around since the 1950's when Dr. John C. Lilly first began experimenting with it. Floating has remained on the fringes, yet is slowly growing in popularity. Several Hollywood movies and TV shows have contained references to it, like Altered States, Minority Report, Stranger Things, the Simpsons, and the Big Bang Theory. In addition, a lot of elite athletes, and famous people are floating. Just go on youtube and search for float therapy to see some of their testimonials.

Because of the increased awareness and the fact that most people that float, fall in love with it, the number of float centers opening around the world has increased. See the google map on the opposite page, for the general locations in the U.S. as of July 2019. There are over 600 in the U.S. alone and they should not be hard to find. Most centers are locally owned and operated, but there are a few franchises. Each center, outside a franchised one, is unique to itself. Some just have floating while others have multiple modalities. The increase in float centers has also lead to an increase in float tank design and sophistication. They even have home float tanks you can buy if you are not near a center, or just want that convenience. Every person is different, so I encourage all floaters to explore different float centers, different types of tanks, different types of owners, atmospheres, memberships, amenities, and find your best fit. To help, you can visit, https://floatationlocations.com/where-to-float/

TAKE AWAYS

Why Do You Want to Float?

_____
_____
_____
_____

What is the Name of Your Closest Float Center?

_____
_____

How Did You Initially Hear About Floating?

_____
_____
_____

General Notes

_____
_____
_____
_____
_____

Getting Ready For Your First Float

PRE-FLOAT PERSONAL ASSESSMENT SPECTRUM

Mark on the line where you think you fall.

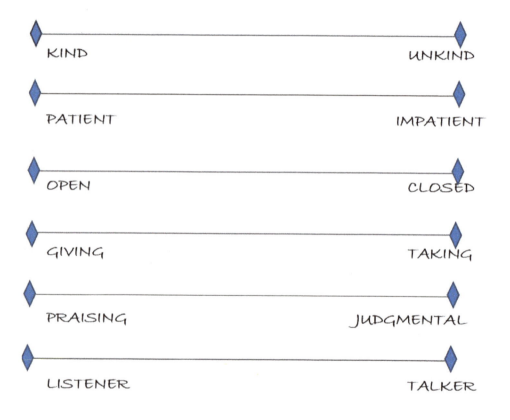

KIND ——————————————————— UNKIND

PATIENT ——————————————————— IMPATIENT

OPEN ——————————————————— CLOSED

GIVING ——————————————————— TAKING

PRAISING ——————————————————— JUDGMENTAL

LISTENER ——————————————————— TALKER

PRE-FLOAT PREPARATION

Before you float your first time, take the personality assessment (opposite) to develop a pre-float baseline. Repeat the assessment after your 3rd and 12th floats to see the changes in your personality. In addition, study the 'quiet the mind' and 'body scanning' techniques on the following pages.

Find your closest float center and book an appointment. Make sure you arrive 15 minutes early to sign any paperwork and get a tour of the facility. See page 19 if you need help.

Avoid Alcohol and Caffeine

Avoid alcohol and drugs before you enter the float tank. Controlled substances already alter the senses. Mixing their influence with floatation may cause you to panic in the float tank, faint, or vomit. You may also begin to experience a hangover in the tank if you drink before a floating session. Since caffeine is a stimulant, you'll want to avoid sodas, coffee, chocolate, and other caffeinated substances before your session as well. These substances increase adrenaline, which makes it harder for your brain to calm down during a floating session.

Most floatation therapies use about a thousand pounds of medical grade Epsom salt per tank to help therapy-goers float. The salt may irritate freshly shaved or waxed areas, so leave your body *au naturel* for a session. Band-Aids will come off in the water, so use liquid bandages for any recent wounds. Some float centers provide single use packets of petroleum jelly that act as a liquid bandage, if needed. Do not float if you have an open wound or rash; it will be painful, and the bacteria may compromise the tank's cleanliness.

Remind Yourself Why You are Floating

Before your appointment, remind yourself why you are floating. Whether it's because of a stressful job, a recent painful event in your family, or generalized anxiety that's difficult to get rid of, knowing why you need floatation therapy will help keep you open to the process. It may help allay some common fears such as claustrophobia as well. Once you know the stressful things you're trying to avoid, it will be easier to consciously tell them to leave your mind during an appointment.

Shower Before and After Floating

Showers help relax the body, which enhances the overall floating experience. Take a cold shower before you get in the tank to hack the mind, and prevent it thinking that you are cold during your float. Most float tanks are heated to around 94 degrees, which is the average person's skin temperature. Taking a cold shower will lower your skin temperature below that, so that when you get in the tank it will feel warm and nice. Always shower after floating since you will be covered in salt solution. Otherwise, your skin can become red and extremely itchy. The float center should provide some ear plugs. I recommend you put them in while taking your first shower because it is easier.

Quieting the Mind

In today's world, we are constantly bombarded with all sorts of stimuli, and rarely get any time alone without any. Floating is a good solution because it puts practitioners in a special environment that removes all outside stimuli, including gravity. However, some people have a very hard time quieting the mind while being alone in an environment like this and will need to work at it.

Mindfulness meditation is a technique a lot of people use to help quiet the mind. The mind is never going to stop thinking, because that is what it does. Therefore, the goal of mindfulness meditation isn't to suppress thinking, but to surpass it. Being mindful means being present and using the whole body as a guide. Once you are present, centered, and here, your mind will naturally quiet down. The techniques below can be used inside a float tank or anywhere that is quiet.

The first step is to get into a comfortable position. For floating, it is mostly about where you put your arms. You can experiment a bit and see what feels most comfortable for you. Then take a deep breath and sigh it out and relax. Close your eyes and focus on listening to your heartbeat and trying to find and focus on the place in your body where you feel your breath most prominently. This is your center. Continue to focus on your center to naturally quiet the mind.

You will have thoughts racing through your head. This in normal. Continue to focus on your breath and heartbeat and try to push those thoughts out of your mind. Later, in the advanced techniques section, we will explain how to screen those thoughts and pay attention to them. But, for now just let them go.

If your mind is still racing, then I recommend you try to visualize something that is calming for you. Similar to the counting sheep technique that you learned as a child to help fall asleep. I like to use the symbol of the Egyptian Ankh (below). It is easy to remember and seems to have a special connection with the soul and symbolizes life or living. If I am really having a hard time quieting the mind, I try to focus in and read the hieroglyphics on the ankh I am visualizing. You don't have to use my example of the ankh, but you are welcome to. Any calming visions will work.

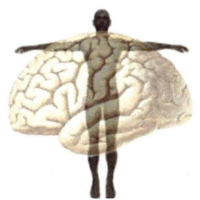

MIND-BODY CONNECTION

Often, the mind-body connection is framed as though the mind and body are two separate systems with their own distinct processes. This is known as dualism. Dualism is the view that the mind and body both exist as separate entities. René Descartes is a famous French mathematician, scientist and philosopher from the 17th century. He argued that there is a two-way interaction between mental and physical substances and that the mind interacts with the body at the pineal gland. This form of dualism (or duality) proposes that the mind controls the body, but that the body can also influence the otherwise rational mind, such as when people act out of passion. Through floating, I have realized that Descartes is right, that the mind and body are intimately interconnected parts of a single unit. Stimulus is processed by the body in equal measure to the mind.

In healing from the past, sometimes the traditional tendency is to focus on the mental narrative. This can be a mistake. While this can be an important aspect of healing, it is important to remember that the body has also suffered the same stress and trauma. By bringing awareness to the sensations of the body and experiencing them fully, these emotional wounds may be healed physically. Sometimes this can even happen without having to go through the process of reliving the bad memories.

While floating, take a few minutes in the beginning to do a body scan. Close your eyes and take several deep breaths. Bring your awareness to the top of your head and move down, slowly taking notice of each part of the body and the sensations present there. Consider that your body is a sentient consciousness communicating with you always. Your body may have intuitive answers to the puzzles and predicaments your mind is trying to solve logically. Have you ever had a gut feeling about something? In some situations, the body's wisdom may prove more beneficial than that of the mind. It is much easier to pay attention to the body in a float tank with external stimuli removed than it is via traditional meditation.

When an emotion surfaces during a float, notice where you feel it in your body. The nervous system is part of the link between the mind and the body. It processes emotions through changes in temperature, heart rate, and physical sensations, to name a few. Becoming aware of these places where changes in the body take place is important and helps calm and reprogram negative emotions. By connecting and integrating all parts of the two systems, you can work to intentionally break down the mental barrier separating the mind consciousness and the body consciousness and can form a cohesive whole or authentic self.

After your float, try to remember what you felt. Note if there were areas of heaviness, lightness, congestion, pain, numbness, tingling, heat, cold, and anything else. Write what you felt in your journal.

There are seven "Chakras" that are considered the energy centers of your body. Chakras connect your spiritual body to your physical one. The word "Chakra" is derived from the Sanskrit word meaning "wheel." Literally translated from the Hindi it means "wheel of spinning energy." A Chakra resembles a whirling, vortex-like, powerhouse of energy. There are seven of these major energy centers within the human body and many more minor ones. Each of the seven is responsible for a specific aspect of your humanity that you can use to cultivate greater harmony, happiness, and well being in your life and in the world. See the chart on the following page.

Chakras regulate the flow of energy throughout the electrical network that runs through the physical body. The body's electrical system resembles the wiring in a house. It allows electrical current to be sent to every part, and it is ready for use when needed. Sometimes these Chakras can become blocked because of stress, emotional, or physical problems. If the body's "energy system" cannot flow freely, it is likely that problems will occur. The consequence of irregular energy flow may be physical illness, discomfort, or a sense of being mentally and emotionally out of balance.

Floating helps unblock your Chakras. The body can purge negative energy in so many ways during a float--by sweating, muscle twitching, aching muscles, yawning, burping, farting, and coughing, to name a few.

When these sensations occur in your body during a float, make a mental note and later try to determine which Chakra is tied to it, and make a note in your journal. If you notice the purging of one Chakra regularly during multiple floats, it might be an indication that the energy blockage may be severe or chronic, and you may need to find a Reiki energy healer to help.

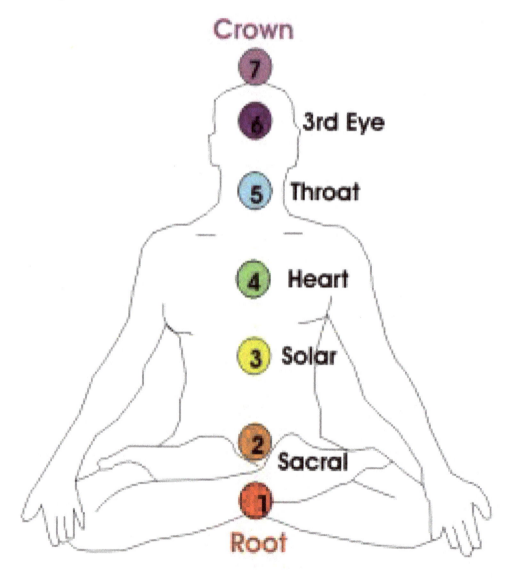

Chakra 7 – The Crown

Its color is violet, and it is located at the top of your head. It is³¹ associated with the cerebral cortex, central nervous system, and the pituitary gland. It is concerned with information, understanding, acceptance, and the feeling of bliss. It is said to be your own place of connection to God-- the Chakra of divine purpose and personal destiny. Blockage can manifest as psychological problems.

Chakra 6 – The Third Eye (or Brow Chakra)

Its color is indigo (a combination of red and blue). It is located at the center of your forehead at eye level or slightly above. This Chakra is used to question the spiritual nature of our life. It is the Chakra of question, perception and knowing. It is concerned with inner vision, intuition and wisdom. Your dreams for this life and recollections of other lifetimes are held in this Chakra. Blockage may manifest as lack of foresight, mental rigidity, "selective" memory, and depression.

Chakra 5. The Throat

Its color is blue or turquoise, and it is located within the throat. it governs the anatomical regions of the thyroid, parathyroid, jaw, neck, mouth, tongue, and larynx. To be open and aligned in the fifth chakra is to speak, listen, and express yourself from a higher form of communication. It is concerned with the senses of inner and outer hearing, the synthesizing of ideas, healing, transformation, and purification. Blockage can show up as creative blocks, dishonesty, or general problems in communicating your needs to others.

Chakra 4 – The Heart

Its color is green, and it is located within your heart. It is the center of love, compassion, harmony and peace. Energy healers say that this is the house of the soul.

The heart Chakra is associated with your lungs, heart, arms, hands and thymus gland. You fall in love through our heart Chakra. Then that feeling of unconditional love moves to the emotional center commonly known as the solar plexus. Blockage can show itself as immune system, lung, and heart problems, or even worse, as inhumanity, lack of compassion or unprincipled behavior.

Chakra 3 – The Solar Plexus

Its color is yellow, and it is located a few inches above the navel in the solar plexus area. This Chakra is concerned with your digestive system, muscles, pancreas, and adrenals. It is the seat of your emotional life. Feelings of personal power, laughter, joy and anger are associated with this center. Your sensitivity, ambition, and ability to achieve are stored here. Blockage may manifest as anger, frustration, lack of direction, or a sense of victimization.

Chakra 2 – The Sacral (or Navel Chakra)

Its color is orange, and it is located between the base of your spine and your navel. It is associated with your lower abdomen, kidneys, bladder, circulatory system and your reproductive organs and glands. It is concerned with emotion. This Chakra represents desire, pleasure, sexuality, procreation and creativity. Blockage may manifest as emotional problems, compulsive or obsessive behavior, and sexual guilt.

Chakra 1 – The Root

Its color is red, and it is located at the perineum or base of your spine. It is the Chakra closest to the earth. Its function is concerned with earthly grounding and physical survival. This Chakra is associated with your legs, feet, bones, large intestine, and adrenal glands. It controls your fight or flight response. Blockage may manifest as paranoia, fear, procrastination, and defensiveness.

Ok, it is time for your first float. Don't think too much about it. You got this. There is a lot of subconscious things that happen in the float tank, so for your first float you just need to focus on getting comfortable in the tank, quieting the mind and doing a body scan. Don't try to do much more. Normally, I advise people to try not to fall asleep during their floats, but for your first float, if you are able to fall asleep it shows that your body and mind were able to get comfortable enough in the tank to trust it. Floating gets easier the more you do it.

Make sure you the follow the recommendations in the "Before You Float" section. You can float wearing whatever you like; however most people float in their birthday suits. You are in your own private room, so there is nothing to worry about. The temperature of the water is the same as your skin temperature, and if done right, you should have a hard time telling where the water begins and your body ends. It all kind of blends in together, and it truly feels like you are floating in outer space or inner space. A swimsuit, can interfere with this sensation and cause you to feel it on your body. So, I recommend everyone float "au natural".

Be careful not to get salt in your eyes. This is really the worst thing that can happen to you in a float. Most times it is self-inflicted, because you go to scratch your noise or forehead and that is how it happens. So, try not to put your hands anywhere near your eyes once you get in the tank. Hopefully, the place you are floating at has something to help relieve the stinging if this happens.

Try to center yourself in the tank, so that you are not touching the walls. You will feel yourself relaxing and getting in the zone, but every time you touch a wall, it will bring you back to reality.

Try to find a comfortable position. Everyone is different so it's hard to say what will work for you. Experiment during your first float, try with your arms at your side, behind your head, out at 90 degrees, over your head, and any variation you can think of. Next move on to your legs, slightly closed or open, 45 degrees open, and so forth. With the help of some noodles, people can even float on their stomachs. This is especially peaceful for pregnant women.

Notice how your neck feels as you are floating. Subconsciously, your body thinks it must hold your neck up in order for you to be able to breathe because this is what it has learned by floating in other bodies of water like rivers, lakes, swimming pools, and the ocean. However, in a float tank it is different, and the salty solution will support your head and neck. But, for some people, they still feel discomfort in their neck, because their body does not trust it. Everyone is different and eventually your body will trust it and this pain goes away. Hopefully, the place where you are floating has a head pillow that will help. If they do, don't start off using that head pillow, wait for the discomfort to kick in, and then use it. And if you use it, try maybe every 15 minutes or so removing it and seeing how your neck feels. Once your body trusts the solution you should never need that neck pillow again, and it feels super relaxing to have your neck resting on the solution alone.

The true magic of floating happens in total darkness where the mind, body, and soul can all interconnect with each other. However, it is your first float, so if you have the option, go slow. Some tanks have lights that can turn colors, or stars on the ceiling. If they have lights, you will be able to control them within the tank. I recommend doing all the previous steps with some light in tank. But once you are comfortable, try turning out some, if not all the lights. If there are stars on the ceiling, maybe leave those on a bit longer to help bring back your childhood memories of gazing up at the stars and pondering what is out there. That helps put your head in the right space. However, at some point during your first float, try it in total darkness.

In some tanks you can have the option of having music pumped into the tank. You can either use your own, or the float center will have its own music. Music may help you relax, but I think of it more as a distraction preventing you from discovering your true self. So, it is really a personal preference. If you want it, make sure you mention it to the float associate.

While you are floating forget about the time, you will be given a signal when your float is over. Hopefully, you will be one of the lucky ones and time will fly by, and you will wonder where it went. For others, each minute can be very uncomfortable if you are not able to quiet the mind and get comfortable in the tank. If that is the case with you, then use the quieting the mind techniques and the body scan technique mentioned previously.

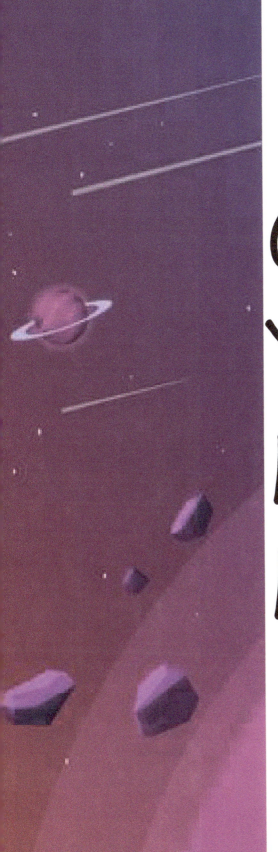

Go Do Your First Float!

AFTER YOUR FLOAT

How was your float? It gets easier the more you do it. You should be feeling pretty good right now, almost like a buzz. That is called the after-float glow. Be careful not to immediately jump right back into the real world. It will seem like it is moving a lot faster if you do. If the float center has a post float lounge, have a seat, make yourself some tea, and just be in the moment for a few minutes. When you are ready, you will want to make a journal entry about how your float was. It is a good habit to get into after every float.

The feelings of relaxation following a float typically last for about 72 hours. Normal things that previously aggravated you won't for the next few days.

After a float, you should be able to sleep soundly for the next few nights. Note the time in the day you floated, because you will find that floating either invigorated you or made you tired. If it invigorated you, then you may want to float in the mornings, and if it made you tired, you may want to float in the evenings.

Any aches and pains you may have felt prior to the float, should have disappeared, and if they have not yet, they will over the next few hours. However, if they are chronic in nature, they will come back after about three days.

Your overall outlook on life will be more positive in nature for the next few days. You will notice more of the beauty in the world around you, within yourself, and within others.

The term "sensory deprivation" has been associated with floating for years. However, it is really not the right term. A more appropriate term is "sensory enhancement". If you were able to go full darkness during your float, then your senses have been kind of reset and enhanced. It is like what happens to the other senses of a blind or deaf person. They become stronger, when one sense is taken away. You may almost feel superhuman after your float: more focus, more creativity, more in touch with the world around you, more attentive, and more in touch with yourself.

Unfortunately, all this is temporary. The feelings will go away after around 72 hours. You will need to get back in and do it again to feel these effects again. Everyone is different so it is hard to generalize how often people should float, but everyone should do it at least once a month, or whenever something stressful in your life is coming up. If you float before the stressful event, and visualize it in your mind in the tank, then it will be a lot less stressful and you will perform better during the actual event.

There is no empirical data to prove it, yet, but I think floaters will live longer with better quality of life because of the reduced stress and positive outlooks that floating brings to their lives. It is kind of naive to say, but if everyone floated every three days the world would be a much more peaceful and happier place.

"Never regret a single moment of the journey. If it wasn't your destination it was your preparation"
-- Unknown

Journaling is a valuable tool when used with floating, as mentioned earlier in this book. There is no right or wrong way to journal, or right or wrong place to do it. You can journal in this guide or you can journal in something else, as long as you are journaling. A sample format is on the facing page. It puts a lot of the basic information at the top so you can easily sort through them and look for patterns, or progress. Some items that you might want to write about are: *how you felt before the float, what you hoped to get out of the float, how you felt after your float, did you achieve what you wanted, what thoughts came into your head during the float, were you comfortable in the tank, did you have any out of body experiences, did you see any past lives, did you declutter your mind any, did you fall asleep, did you work through any trauma, did you notice your body or mind trying to tell you something, did you relive any early child hood experiences, etc....* just write what comes to you.

FIRST FLOAT JOURNAL ENTRY

Date of Float:	Time of Float	Place of Float:
Type of Tank:	Full Sensory Deprivation?	Length of Float:
Pre-Float Intentions?	Techniques Used	Overall Experience

_____

_____

_____

_____

_____

_____

_____

_____

_____

_____

_____

_____

_____

_____

_____

_____

_____

_____

_____

_____

SEVEN THOUGHTS ON FLOATING

1. Make peace with your past so it does not affect the present.

2. What others think of you is none of your business.

3. Time heals almost everything, so give it time.

4. Don't compare your life to others and don't judge them. You have no idea what their journey is about.

5. It's alright not to know all the answers. They will come to you when you are ready.

6. You are in charge of your own happiness, so spend some time with yourself.

7. Smile. You don't own all the problems in the world.

INTERMEDIATE
TECHNIQUES TO PREPARE
FOR YOUR SECOND FLOAT.

What is the
difference between
Loneliness and
Solitude?
Float therapy!
- cl jones

INTENTIONS

Having an intention can be helpful in navigating a float experience. It is like sailing the sea with a compass. Using a compass doesn't mean you are limiting yourself to a plan or set route; it means you will have a sense of direction and clarity. You probably did not realize it, but by using this guide, you had an intention for your first float, which was to just get comfortable in the tank. When you have a clear intention, you are giving your subconscious a direction to work in. Set your intentions before a float but release your attachment to the outcome. Allow the intentions to be your compass but not your map.

You can also approach a float without an intention, having faith that your mind, body, and soul will give you the experience that you need.

In either scenario, you may encounter a flood of input or nothing at all, and that is perfectly okay.

Intentions vs Expectations

Intentions and expectations are <u>not</u> the same thing, and it is easy for one to turn into the other. Being mindful and open will help your intention unfold. Having pre-determined expectations for the float can hinder your ability to let go and trust the process. Sometimes trying to exercise control can lead to a difficult, frightening or unpleasant experience. Learn that you are not really in control and learn to accept that.

Expectation is the root of all heartache.
-- William Shakespeare

It is important to note that floating can sometimes work in subtle ways, such as through intuition or dream-like thoughts. Some people do not experience visions. Try to practice non-judgment and trust the mind, body, soul process is happening whether you can perceive the effects or not. Insights may arise in the following days or weeks. Sometimes your body just needs to relax and unwind, and you won't experience any insights. Trust that it will give you what you need, even if that is only to relax.

Some **non-specific** examples of Intentions for a Float:
- I release that which no longer serves me.
- I want to find direction and open my path.
- I'm here to understand and heal my anxiety.

Some **specific** examples of Intentions for a Float:
- I release the stress and anxiety associated with....
- I want to understand and embrace my true self.
- I just want to relax.
- I want to understand if I am truly happy.
- I want to declutter my mind.
- I want to see the results of next week's lotto drawing 😊

REFRAMING

When facing stress, the way stressors are viewed can have a huge impact on the perceived ability to overcome and persevere through obstacles. Reframing is a technique used to challenge negative/overwhelming thoughts to create a perspective where the same truth is expressed, but from an empowered position. To reframe a negative thought is not to suggest the original thought is false or mistaken, it is to approach the circumstance from a different perspective and verbalize it in another way. When using reframing as a tool, remember to have compassion for yourself. Recognize that changing negative thoughts can be a difficult process.

This is how you need to retrain yourself to think in the tank. Some common examples of negative thoughts while floating are identified in the chart below.

Negative Thoughts	Re-Framed Thoughts
I can't let go	I am still learning how to let go
I am all alone	Alone is a safe place from which I can reach out for help from within
I don't know what I want to do with my life	I have a lot of passions and abilities to discover

Practical Exercise:
Try reframing some of your persistent negative thoughts.

THE POWER OF WORDS

Words and thoughts have the potential to create your reality. We all have well-established habits of the mind that are both healthy and unhealthy. The accumulation of speed, self-talk, and thought is influential at the subconscious level. Changing the way you think takes time, especially when a narrative has been forming for years. Incorporate the reframing technique previously discussed to positively speak to yourself.

Using a mantra or affirmation that you resonate with can remind you that you are not your mind and that you have the power to influence your reality. Life is not happening to you, rather you are a participant in the experience. Spending a few minutes during a float, or outside of a float, reciting a mantra out loud can help bring the truth of the words into your daily life. You can also choose to write a phrase down and display it someplace where you will see it regularly. When you speak the words of your mantra or affirmation, consciously bring forth and experience the associated positive emotions in your body.

Examples of Positive Affirmations:
- I trust my floating process.
- I am worthy of love.
- May all beings be happy.
- May all beings be healthy.
- May all beings be at peace.
- I honor my progress.
- This too shall pass.

Find your own Mantras that are positive in nature and resonate with you!

"Be impeccable with your word. Speak with integrity. Say only what you mean. Avoid using the word to speak against yourself or to gossip about others. Use the power of your word in the direction of truth and love."
--Don Miguel Ruiz, The Four Agreements

YOUR SECOND FLOAT

You should do your second float within about 10 days of your first float, if not sooner, and not later than 30 days. This way your conscious and subconscious mind will remember everything they learned on your first float. Because of that, your second float should be easier. Make sure you review everything in this guide about your first float, quieting your mind, and your body scan techniques. It is a good idea, to re-read your first journal entry.

If you liked the type of float tank you were in on your first float, then you can stay in the same tank. However, if your float center has multiple types, and you felt claustrophobic or wrote something else in your journal about the tank that was bothering you, then maybe you should try another type of tank or float center. Floating can be hard enough in the beginning without your subconscious sabotaging you, and if something bothered you on your first float, it may continue if you don't do something about it.

The same goes for the time frame of the float, if it was too long, or too short, now is the time to change it up. Everyone is different, and there is some evidence to show that a 90-minute float aligns nicely with your natural ultradian rhythm. The ultradian rhythm is a 90-120 minute cycle that is your optimized rest-activity sequence that corresponds to different levels of energy and alertness. Recent float surveys find most people prefer a 60-minute float the best. Figure out what works best for you and you may need to slowly work up to it.

You have learned some new tools to use in your second float. All the tools provided to you so far are really the foundation of what you need to get the most out of your floatation experience. You just need to practice and start honing your skills. It gets easier the more you do it. These tools will continue to build on themselves. You may need to use bits and pieces of each, depending on what is going on with you in the tank. All these skills can also be used outside a float tank. For example, if you are sitting in traffic and getting more and more frustrated, close your eyes and remember your float experience. Take some deep breaths and just relax. The feeling will come back to you and put you back into a state of zen.

For your second float, you should set an intention similar to what you unintentionally set for your first float. Something like, **"I am still learning to get comfortable and let go."** Go slow. You will have many floats after this one when you can start to explore the depths of who you are. For now, just focus on continuing to get comfortable in the tank. Work on training your mind to think positive thoughts while you float using what you learned in the reframing process and the "Power of Words" sections. You should get into the zone much quicker and stay there longer on your second float.

Enjoy It!

Go Float For Your Second Time!

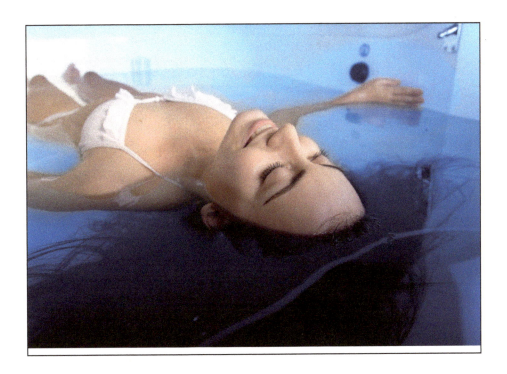

Refer to the "After-Your-Float" section to recall what to expect. (Pages 38-39)

Remember to journal after your float. You do not need to journal immediately afterward, but don't put it off so long that you have forgotten what you experienced.

Just as in your journal entries after your first float, some items you might want to write about are: *how you felt before the float, what you hoped to get out of the float, how you felt after your float, did you achieve what you wanted, what thoughts came into your head during the float, were you comfortable in the tank, did you have any out-of-body experiences, did you see any past lives, did you declutter your mind any, did you fall asleep, did you work through any trauma, did you notice your body or mind trying to tell you something, did you relive any early child hood experiences, etc....* just write what comes to you.

SECOND FLOAT JOURNAL ENTRY

Date of Float:	Time of Float	Place of Float:
Type of Tank:	Full Sensory Deprivation?	Length of Float:
Pre-Float Intentions?	Techniques Used	Overall Experience

_____

_____

_____

_____

_____

_____

_____

_____

_____

_____

_____

_____

_____

_____

_____

_____

_____

_____

_____

_____

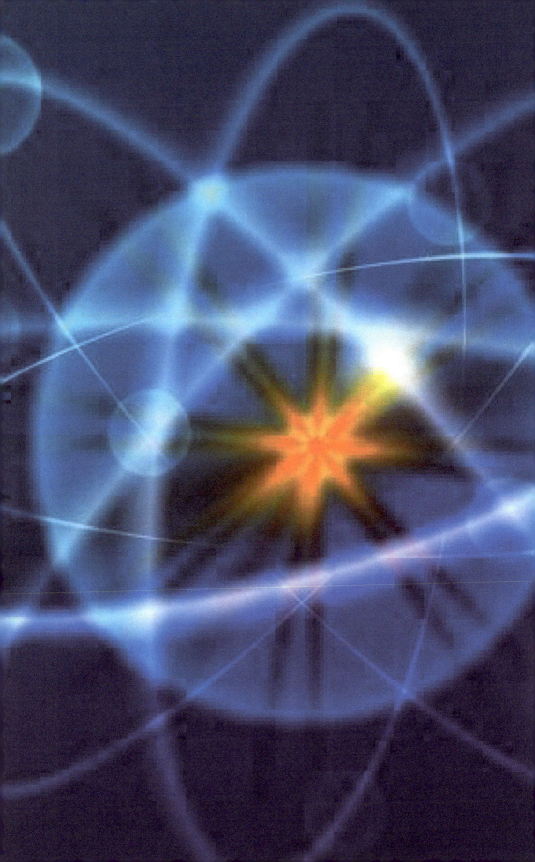

ADVANCED TECHNIQUES TO PREPARE FOR YOUR THIRD FLOAT AND BEYOND

THE OUROBOROS

The ouroboros, a snake or dragon depicted eating its own tail, is an image used widely among many cultures to represent the cyclical nature of the universe. It reflects the cycles all beings are constantly moving through. Everyone has the opportunity to recognize these patterns in themselves, learn their lessons, and transform the cycles with each new iteration. The illustration below explores the symbolic representation of this process.

Spring, Creation, Rebirth

An incredible amount of energy is bursting forth with newness. This is a good time to set intentions.

Summer, Growth, Manifestation

Intentions and awareness translate into action. Momentum moves forward. You are faced with the lessons of your cycle.

Winter, Destruction, Death

Give permission for the cycle to end. Allow room for grieving and celebration. The lessons of this cycle are the foundation for the next. Breathe and make room for what will follow.

Fall, Reflection, Integration

Momentum slows, and there is space to observe. This can feel like stagnation, but recognize patterns and allow the lessons to sink in.

While floating, complete the following statements, and try to get insights and learn from the ouroboros:

-- An example of a healthy cycle playing out in my life is...

-- A cycle I am feeling trapped in is....

-- The stage where I feel I am in this cycle is...

Then ask yourself the following questions:

-- What would I like to change about my cycle?

-- Have I noticed any patterns?

First Fight · Injury · Stress · loss · Death · Humility · Failure · Prom · Love · Mistakes · Lost Virginity · success · Birth · heartbreak

All life's experiences are metaphorically stored in boxes in the closet that is our mind. We don't remember what's in half of them.

DECLUTTERING THE MIND

Each experience you have in life is stored in your body and mind. Depending how old you are, the storage area can get quite extensive. Your mind is like a metaphorically overstuffed closest containing boxes of different sizes and shapes each box containing one experience. Most people don't even remember what is in most of those boxes, but they clutter their minds, slowing them down and keeping them from achieving their full potential.

Occasionally, something happens in life that causes one of those boxes to accidentally fall off the shelf and spill all over the floor. This is what happens when people have panic attacks, go crazy, or lose their minds in public. Something triggers something deep inside one of those boxes causing its content to spill out-- sometimes at a most inopportune time.

Floating can help declutter the mind. Set an intention before each float to declutter your mind. You don't have to know which box you should open. Let your subconscious guide you to a box. Once you have it, open it, and pay attention to the vision or lesson inside. You may have to selectively screen out some of your thoughts almost as if you are dreaming but are able to control the dream. For instance, if a cheeseburger comes into your mind, you may want to push it aside, and see what else comes. Perhaps the cheeseburger might be the start of reliving an experience that took place at a barbeque, or it might also just mean you are hungry. If it means the latter, push it aside and look for more. The more you do it, the more you will learn what to look for.

It might take a while to figure out what the revelation is, but when you do, work to try to find out what the lesson is, or why it is even in the box stored away in your mind in the first place. You will be re-looking at the experience almost in the third person. During the float, while watching the experience, try to forgive yourself or the other person if the vision is about something someone did to you. If, on the other hand, it is something that does not pertain directly to you, but is something you witnessed, then forgive yourself as you could have done nothing to affect the outcome. You just happened to be in the wrong place at the wrong time. In all these cases, let the experience go. Through acknowledging one of these three things, the box should disappear from your mind. You will emerge from your float feeling as if you are lighter because you have eliminated one box from your closet.

Continue to work to declutter your mind. It may never be fully clean, but you will be releasing things that no longer serve you, and you will be healthier for it. Don't worry about encountering frightening things. Your subconscious will never let you open a box that you are not yet ready to handle. All the negative energy in a lot of those boxes affects your health in so many destructive ways, so decluttering the mind is very important.

Reliving trauma is never fun for anyone, and it is important to be aware that trauma can surface while floating. Understanding more about what it is and the ways it can be brought forward can help prepare you if trauma surfaces. Sometimes it can be called forth via purposeful intentions, other times it surfaces out of the blue. Either way, understand that your mind, body, and soul won't give you more than you can handle in a float until you're ready.

From a shamanistic point of view, most illnesses and diseases are manifestations of blockages or "knots" in the energy of a person where excess or insufficient energy creates imbalance in the overall mind, body, soul, system. Such blockages often happens throughout a person's life as a result of trauma in its various forms. Shock trauma-- often the result of abuse, attack, or loss – is the most common form, but trauma can result from many common life occurrences. Examples include surgery, accidents, illness, injuries, financial difficulties, cultural and societal pressures, betrayal or anger from relationships just to name a few.

Using the decluttering techniques while floating will help you to rebalance your energy. Once your energy is rebalanced, your body will have an easier time healing.

Often, victims of trauma do not realize the full impact of the past event(s) as the effects are long lasting and can become part of the individual's everyday existence. The real weight of trauma is not necessarily in the experiencing of the traumatic event(s), but in their extended suffering following the initial circumstance. The nervous system holds onto the state of hyper or hypo arousal, sending the body a message that the traumatic event is still in progress. Over time, this takes its toll on the body and mind, hindering your ability to participate fully in the present moment. Trauma can manifest as symptoms such as unpredictable emotions, flashbacks, strained relationships, addictions, and even physical symptoms like headaches or nausea. Trauma can also become a contributing factor in many other diseases.

While floating is an incredible tool that helps the human condition with so many things, recognize that it is just that, a tool. It should not be used alone when dealing with trauma. It should be integrated with other tools (like therapy) for best results. Floating will enable you to evoke and relive past experiences with visions, some good and some bad.

The various manifestations of trauma just discussed can hold you back from reaching your full potential. When they happen, they are a sign, that you need to deal with it. Previously subconscious memories of the traumas or new details about them can surface during a float and when this happens, the process can be cathartic.

Floating can help you fully acknowledge things the body has long held onto. These include emotions, sensations, and unreleased energy. Floating helps you relive that trauma in almost a third-person reality, as if you are watching it unfold on a TV screen. The emotions will still be present, but they will be less personal. This helps you realize that what happened to you, does not define you, and allows you to cope with the experience better.

Viewing a trauma in a new way can make space for compassion and forgiveness. Individuals who have experienced abuse sometimes report that this compassion can even extend to understanding their perpetrator's suffering and, in some cases, forgiving them. Self-blame and regret may be released, and self-forgiveness may emerge enabling floaters to love themselves despite the trauma inflicted on them or by them.

SHADOW WORK

The shadow represents the parts of the self kept in the darkness, out of sight. These aspects of the self have been pushed away because they are difficult to look at. These unexamined or disowned pieces are repressed because they are perceived as unacceptable, evil, or undesirable. Parts of the shadow often stems from childhood when a situation or reaction taught you that these thoughts or experiences were wrong or bad.

The psychologist Carl Jung, and I paraphrase, felt that having a shadow is part of what makes people human. It can manifest as an expression of not only your personal darkness, but also as a collective cultural darkness. He felt that everyone carries a shadow, and the less it is embodied in your conscious life, the blacker, and denser it is. At all counts, it forms an unconscious snag, thwarting your most well-meant intentions. Jung went on to say that the shadow is a moral problem that challenges the whole ego-personality, for you cannot become conscious of the shadow without considerable moral effect. Becoming conscious of it involves recognizing the dark aspects of your personality as present and real. This act is the essential condition for any kind of self-knowledge, and therefore, as a rule, meets with considerable resistance. Floating naturally helps reduce that resistance because it eliminates all your external senses, making it easier to connect with your mind, body, and soul which subconsciously interacts with our shadow all the time.

Facing the shadow, accepting the shadow, and integrating the shadow can all be very intense work. This introspective method, when undertaken, is a maturation process. The resultant transformation requires you to stop self-suppression and engage life with fuller authenticity. It is not uncommon that shadow work can emerge while floating, and if it does, embrace it. Don't fear it, even though it may be painful. Other tools, like therapy, along with floating can be used to make it easier.

How much do I actually know about my shadow?

EGO DEATH

This is one of the most advanced techniques discussed in floatosophy and can be the hardest and the most painful to experience, but it offers the greatest potential for true happiness. There are many tools you can use to help you experience an ego death, or loss of your sense of self and identity. These include yoga, psychedelic plant medicines, meditation, and floating. In order to experience an ego death while floating, you will need to use portions of every technique you have learned in this guide.

The death of the ego isn't truly a death, as the ego will always be a part of you. Instead, it's more like a transcendence. You evolve beyond the shackles of your ego and leave it behind, learning to control your life without its influence. When you leave behind the ego in an ego death you return to your *True Nature* and learn to live beyond the confines of your ego's dualistic reality.

This experience can be both beautiful and terrifying, depending on how ready you are to let go of your ego. This complete loss of identity can be the most petrifying experience ever because your ego's defense mechanism may try to kick in to keep itself attached to you, which often times actually feels like you are dying. This is why it is referred to as an ego death.

"One way to think about ego is as a protective heavy shell, such as the kind some animals have, like a big beetle. This protective shell works like armor to cut you off from other people and the outside world. What I mean by shell is a sense of separation: Here's me and there's the rest of the universe and other people. The ego likes to emphasize the "otherness" of others."
-- Eckhart Tolle

To work to experience an ego death while floating you need to become aware of your ego, explore the unknown, learn from it, and surrender to it. This is the path of knowledge or *Jnana Yoga* in Eastern cultures. The big problem with the ego is that it loves to strengthen itself through negativity. When you listen to the ego and its negativity, it starts to control you and how you behave. To help combat this, previous chapters of floatosophy have taught you how to reframe your thoughts, and how to use positive affirmations while floating.

After several floats, you will begin to have out-of-body experiences, if you let yourself. It starts with feeling a sense of falling, spinning, or flying. This is you trying to pull away from your ego or sense of self. At first many try to resist it, because it is uncomfortable, but if you want to experience an ego death, then you need to embrace it. To help, begin the float asking yourself "Who am I really" and use all the techniques you have previously read about. It may start subtly, with visions of clouds or colors or something similar. Begin to focus on those images and what you are feeling. Then focus more and just let go. Go where it takes you. During and after your experience, try to learn from it and eventually surrender to it. Don't worry. You will always come back. It may take years to fully be able to surrender to it and become one with the universe. When it happens, you realize that who you are is something so much greater.

Positives Associated with an Ego Death

1) You experience many positive feelings.

2) You see yourself for who you really are. You see what you don't like about yourself and will know what you can change to make yourself a better person.

3) You experience emotions you are not able to feel normally because of your ego. You are becoming in touch with your whole being.

4) You change the way you view the world. You won't be clouded by your ego's insecurities and desires.

5) You experience feelings you haven't felt since you were a child. You begin to experience a pure mind.

Negatives Associated with an Ego Death

1) You may see yourself for who you are, and you won't be protected by your ego. This can be frightening and uncomfortable.

2) You might experience feelings and emotions that you've been hiding from for years.

3) You see yourself as a different person, without the insecurities (or securities) of your ego. to hide behind. If you've been using your ego for protection, this can be shattering.

4) You may feel disappointed in who you've been.

5) You may undergo a psychological transformation that changes your thought patterns.

You should do your third float within about ten days of your second for the same reasons mentioned earlier. The third float is really the magic number and should be your best float to date. Your mind, body, and soul should now be comfortable floating, and you should begin to see some real benefits. (page 38,39)

Read your previous journal entries. Repetition is supposedly the mother of all learning, so try to repeat everything that has worked for you so far. If some things have not worked, then change it up.

The last section went into some real advanced techniques to be used with floating to help you discover your true self. None of them need to be used in your third float. And in fact, they should probably not be used until you have mastered the basics that you practiced during for your first two floats. It is okay not to go into the advanced techniques. Sometimes feeling good is all you really need. And you will feel fabulous after your third float.

When you are ready and want to begin using some of the advanced tools, you should start with decluttering the mind, and repeat that multiple times as you float. It will free up some space and energy and help increase your vibration, which will allow you to go further. Your mind, body, and soul will bring the others to the forefront---but only, when you are ready.

How often you continue to float is up to you. Everyone
has different levels of stress in their lives, different
schedules and availability, and different financial
capabilities. However, remind yourself why you started
floating in the first place and review what it has done for
you so far. You can use the personality assessment on
the next page to help.

Regardless of your situation, floating should be
incorporated into your lifestyle because it will make you
a happier, healthier, human being. The body is
amazing, and if you give it the proper tools, like floating,
it will help heal itself without the aid of pharmaceuticals.

Enjoy the journey, the possibilities are endless.

Go Do Your Third Float and Continue to Float On!

POST- 3 FLOAT PERSONAL ASSESSMENT SPECTRUM

Mark on the line where you think you fall.

KIND ←——————————————————————→ UNKIND

PATIENT ←——————————————————————→ IMPATIENT

OPEN ←——————————————————————→ CLOSED

GIVING ←——————————————————————→ TAKING

PRAISING ←——————————————————————→ JUDGMENTAL

LISTENER ←——————————————————————→ TALKER

Compare with your pre-float Assessment. What do you think?

_____

_____

_____

_____

_____

_____

Do you prefer this one?

Date of Float:	Time of Float	Place of Float:
Type of Tank:	Full Sensory Deprivation?	Length of Float:
Pre-Float Intentions?	Techniques Used	Overall Experience

"A~~n apple~~{float} a day keeps the doctor away."

— ~~Benjamin Franklin~~ Christopher L. Jones

TARGETED FLOAT TECHNIQUES

Visualization. A lot of successful people use floating as a tool to prepare them for something stressful in their future. They float to help them perform better or achieve their goal. It is very similar to the law of attraction. Set your intention to something like: "I want to see what is going to happen ..." and then float on it. Clear your mind of everything else and visualize the event in your head. For example, this technique can be used when you have a big stressful event like a wedding, an important test like the SAT, or a very important business meeting coming up. Float before the event and visualize whatever it is that may cause you stress. You will perform better and be less stressed when it happens. The more times you can float before the event the better off you will be.

Addiction. Floating can help with addiction, but it should only be used after a formal detox period, as a tool, to help change patterns and help prevent relapse. You will need access to a float tank at all hours of the day and night because you need to float whenever the urge to do or use whatever you are addicted to comes on. For most, after your float, you will no longer have the desire to do or use whatever you are addicted to. Everyone is different, but the feeling should last between 24-72 hours. You will also feel better about yourself and be able to forgive yourself, giving you the strength to keep going. When the urge comes on again, get back in the tank. Keep repeating until the urge no longer returns. This technique should be used with other traditional solutions like attending regular support meetings and changing other bad habits.

Post-Traumatic Stress Disorder (PTSD). Steve Maraboli, author of *Unapologetically You: Reflections on Life and the Human Experience* says that "The truth is, unless you let go, unless you forgive yourself, unless you forgive the situation, unless you realize that the situation is over, you cannot move forward." This has been true in my experience with PTSD. To keep your PTSD at bay, you probably need to float at least once a week or whenever you start to feel the signs come on. Review all the techniques mentioned throughout this guide as you will need to incorporate pieces of them all to help overcome the symptoms of PTSD. You will need to work on forgiving yourself, forgiving the other people involved, or forgiving the situation. You will also need to work on relaxation to help balance your fight or flight response and your rest and relaxation response. Most people with PTSD have developed the bad habit of operating in the fight or flight mode predominantly. Their nervous systems need to be recalibrated so that they can operate more in the rest and relaxation mode. Floating will automatically help with that recalibration.

Depression/Suicidal thoughts. You need to get in the tank and float any time you are depressed and/or you have suicidal thoughts.You probably need to float about six times in a ten-day period to fully break away from those thoughts, but you should feel better immediately after your first float. If you recall from the post-float section, floating helps you view the world and yourself in a much more positive light. Items that seemed insurmountable before a float come into perspective, and either are not that important anymore, or they have become achievable. If the depression or suicidal thoughts continue, you should probably seek some professional counseling. There is a National Suicide Prevention lifeline **1-800-273-8255** if you need immediate help.

Past Life Regression. Floating can help you see past lives. Set your intention to something like: "To see and understand who I really am." Remember the chapter about the Ouroboros and life and multiple lifetime cycles. If you can visualize your past life, you may be able to see patterns, learn universal lessons, deal with past life trauma, and better understand where and who you are in the big picture. The effectiveness of this tool can be enhanced if you have someone experienced in past life regression to talk to in conjunction with floating.

Early and Pre-birth thoughts. Floating is the closest thing to being in your mother's womb, so it is the perfect environment for remembering early memories. Set your intention to: "Remember my earliest thoughts of childhood" and float on it. Each time you will remember or visualize something from your childhood. You will start at around four or five years old but will be able keep going back further and further the more you do it. You will be surprised by how far you can go back. In theory, eventually you should be able to remember your pre-birth thoughts and emotions and learn from them. So much of who you are was shaped unintentionally early on in your life by your parents and loved ones. This technique will help you better understand your loved ones' actions and how you responded to them—perhaps even furthering feelings of love and compassion for them.

Integration with other Modalities. Float therapy works just[79] fine as a stand-alone solution to many problems. However, if it is integrated with other modalities, its results can be intensified. Some modalities that work well with floating are infra-red saunas, red light therapy, acupuncture, massage, light therapy, magnetic resonance therapy, acoustical sound therapy, cryogenics, Reiki, and many more. It is best to try each of these modalities separately in the beginning, as each will affect everyone differently. It is important to understand what each does specifically for you. Otherwise, if you start out with an infrared sauna, light therapy, and float therapy stack, you may feel absolutely great. But you will need to complete that stack every time in the future to achieve the same results; whereas, maybe only light therapy and floating had the greatest impact on you. If that was the case, you can do away with the infra-red sauna and save yourself some time and money.

In addition, as mentioned before, traditional western medical solutions can often help intensify your float experience, so I would make sure you talk to your doctor if you want to integrate floating into your traditional healing process.

Make it a tradition: honor the experience of your birth and float on your birthday!

Famous Floaters

To help provide you some motivation and inspiration to keep floating and prove to you that you are in good company. Below is a list of famous people who float. They are in no specific order:

Stephen Curry is one of the most famous players on the Golden State Warriors basketball team. The writers at *Men's Journal* and other news sources speculate that floating may be behind his incredible athletic performance.

Michael Crichton (author, "Westworld") found floating at a crucial time in his career and claimed that the practice helped cure him of writer's block.

Singer/songwriter **John Lennon** of the Beatles reported floating helped him kick his heroin habit in the late 1970s. He also reported feeling healthier than he ever felt.

Elle Macpherson: (Supermodel) Has has touted the benefits of floating and its magnesium-rich Epsom salts for skin and beauty care.

Best-selling author **Tim Ferriss** touts floating as "one of the most anxiety-reducing experiences I've ever had"– and as a tool towards the rapid acquisition of new knowledge.

Carl Lewis. (Olympic Athlete) When he was preparing for his gold-medal-winning runs at the Seoul Olympics in 1988, he used floatation therapy extensively for the purpose of visualization.

Actress and comedian **Kristen Wiig** is another frequent floater. She has spoken with David Letterman about her experiences and particularly touts how great her skin feels after a session.

Wayne Rooney. Manchester United's Midfielder actually owns a float tank, allowing him to spend as many as 10 hours a week floating.

Tom Brady, QB for the New England Patriots, winner of 5 Superbowl's. Tom doesn't just use the tank for healing his sports injuries or for the sake of the skin benefits of the Epsom Salt, he transformed the floatation therapy into a powerful meditation ritual that helps him to maintain a strong and focused mindset and to deeply relax his mind.

Jeff Bridges.(Actor) He meditates daily and was a close friend of the inventor of the sensory deprivation tank or 'float tank', Dr John C. Lilly. Lilly used Bridges as an early test subject in his initial experiments with the isolation tanks in the 1970's making him an early float tank pioneer.

UFC Host, Taekwondo & Brazilian Jiu-Jitsu black belt, and Fear Factor Host **Joe Rogan** owns his own float tank and talks about the affects of floating on his popular podcasts.

Rachel Hunter is a successful supermodel who hails from New Zealand. She's also a fan of float therapy and meditation. When asked to describe her experience in the float tank, she shared that "it was a bizarrely delightful experience, a great form of meditation. I felt calm and peaceful, yet energized…"

Willie Mason. (Rugby NRL legend) is a regular floater. Mason has credited his time in float pods as being a powerful recovery tool.

Silver Medalist in 2008 Beijing Olympics, British Triple Jumper **Phillips Idowu**, used floatation therapy weekly for a back injury.

Swedish professional freeskier and alpine ski racer, 9-time Winter X game medalist, **Jon Olsson** keeps on top of his game with floating.

MMA fighter **Pat Healy** has credited his wins to his float practice, while **Royce Gracie** and **Pedro Sauer** float regularly.

Lennox Lewis. (Boxer) is one of greatest boxers of all time and part of the boxing hall of fame. He says that he used the floating in an isolation tank as a post-workout routine that helped him to better control his mind and as a 'treatment' for sore muscles.

Michael Phelps. (Olympic Athlete) The former competition swimmer has the impressive 28 medals. He broke every important record in several disciplines, thus stunning the world every time he participated in the Olympics. The floatation therapy is an important aspect of his meditation and relaxation and he claims that this method of well-being still helps him to achieve inner peace.

Gerard Mousasi. The Iranian-born MMA star Gerard Mousasi is currently a Bellator Middleweight World Champion. Fight Matrix ranks him as the number four middleweight MMA fighter in the world. Mousasi credits the floating in a sensory deprivation tank as his primary tool for recovery, stress-relief, and concentration.

Other notable floaters

Robin Williams. Actor, Comedian.

Jim Carrey, Actor, Comedian

Susan Sarandon, Actor

Russell Brand, Actor, Comedian

Neil Young, Singer, Songwriter

Drew Carey, Comedian, Host of Price is Right

JJ Watt, NFL Defensive Player of the Year, Houston Texans

Russell Wilson, QB for the Seattle Seahawks

Peter Gabriel, Singer, Songwriter

Julian Edelman. Receiver for the New England Patriots

US Special Forces Operators

Many College and Professional Sports teams

And there are many more...

Continue to Float and Journal using everything you have learned.

FLOAT JOURNAL ENTRY

Date of Float:	Time of Float	Place of Float:
Type of Tank:	**Full Sensory Deprivation?**	**Length of Float:**
Pre-Float Intentions?	**Techniques Used**	**Overall Experience**

_____

_____

_____

_____

_____

_____

_____

_____

_____

_____

_____

_____

_____

_____

_____

_____

_____

_____

_____

FLOAT JOURNAL ENTRY

Date of Float:	Time of Float	Place of Float:
Type of Tank:	Full Sensory Deprivation?	Length of Float:
Pre-Float Intentions?	Techniques Used	Overall Experience

_____

_____

_____

_____

_____

_____

_____

_____

_____

_____

_____

_____

_____

_____

_____

_____

_____

_____

_____

FLOAT JOURNAL ENTRY

Date of Float:	Time of Float	Place of Float:
Type of Tank:	Full Sensory Deprivation?	Length of Float:
Pre-Float Intentions?	Techniques Used	Overall Experience

_____

_____

_____

_____

_____

_____

_____

_____

_____

_____

_____

_____

_____

_____

_____

_____

_____

_____

_____

FLOAT JOURNAL ENTRY

Date of Float:	Time of Float	Place of Float:
Type of Tank:	Full Sensory Deprivation?	Length of Float:
Pre-Float Intentions?	Techniques Used	Overall Experience

_____
_____
_____
_____
_____
_____
_____
_____
_____
_____
_____
_____
_____
_____
_____
_____
_____
_____

FLOAT JOURNAL ENTRY

Date of Float:	Time of Float	Place of Float:
Type of Tank:	Full Sensory Deprivation?	Length of Float:
Pre-Float Intentions?	Techniques Used	Overall Experience

_____

_____

_____

_____

_____

_____

_____

_____

_____

_____

_____

_____

_____

_____

_____

_____

_____

_____

_____

FLOAT JOURNAL ENTRY

Date of Float:	Time of Float	Place of Float:
Type of Tank:	Full Sensory Deprivation?	Length of Float:
Pre-Float Intentions?	Techniques Used	Overall Experience

_____
_____
_____
_____
_____
_____
_____
_____
_____
_____
_____
_____
_____
_____
_____
_____
_____
_____
_____
_____

FLOAT JOURNAL ENTRY

Date of Float:	Time of Float	Place of Float:
Type of Tank:	Full Sensory Deprivation?	Length of Float:
Pre-Float Intentions?	Techniques Used	Overall Experience

_____

_____

_____

_____

_____

_____

_____

_____

_____

_____

_____

_____

_____

_____

_____

_____

_____

_____

FLOAT JOURNAL ENTRY

Date of Float:	Time of Float	Place of Float:
Type of Tank:	Full Sensory Deprivation?	Length of Float:
Pre-Float Intentions?	Techniques Used	Overall Experience

FLOAT JOURNAL ENTRY

Date of Float:	Time of Float	Place of Float:
Type of Tank:	Full Sensory Deprivation?	Length of Float:
Pre-Float Intentions?	Techniques Used	Overall Experience

_____

_____

_____

_____

_____

_____

_____

_____

_____

_____

_____

_____

_____

_____

_____

_____

_____

_____

_____

_____

_____

INNER BEAUTY

You should be an expert floater by now. Take the last personal assessment test opposite and compare the results from the first two.

POST-12 FLOAT PERSONAL ASSESSMENT SPECTRUM

Mark on the line where you think you fall.

KIND ◆————————————————◆ UNKIND

PATIENT ◆————————————————◆ IMPATIENT

OPEN ◆————————————————◆ CLOSED

GIVING ◆————————————————◆ TAKING

PRAISING ◆————————————————◆ JUDGMENTAL

LISTENER ◆————————————————◆ TALKER

Compare with your previous assessments. What do you think?

_____

_____

_____

_____

_____

Are you becoming a better person?

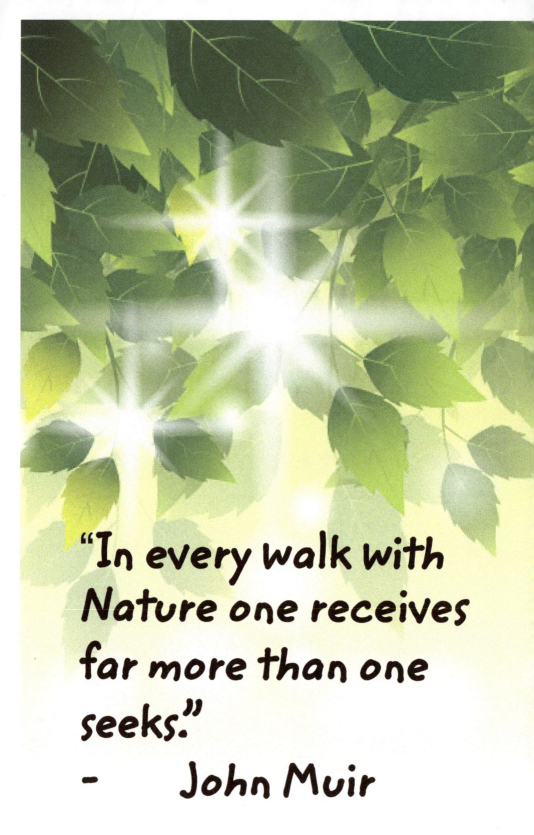

"In every walk with Nature one receives far more than one seeks."

\-   John Muir

WINNING COMBINATION

To enhance the floatation experience and reflect, I like to take a walk in nature after my float. The beauty of nature becomes more pronounced after a float. M. Amos Clifford created a similar guide to this one called "*Forest Bathing*", that when used in conjunction with floating will provide you even more healing power and a greater sense of the universe and mother nature. He reveals the ancient secrets of the of Japanese Shinrin-Yoku to you.

Interactive Resources

www.nfifa.org The National Float It Forward Association, providing free floatation therapy to active military, veterans, first responders, and their immediate families.

www.floatlocations.com The place to go to find resources on floating and where to find your nearest float center worldwide.

www.clinicalfloatation.com The place to go to find news and clinical studies on floatation therapy.

National Suicide Prevention Lifeline: **1-800-273-8255**

https://youtu.be/_S90KoTlDWw Joe Rogan YouTube Find Yourself Video approx. 5 minutes in length

https://youtu.be/nHnbKjQGhHw Float Nation Documentary on YouTube 1 approx 1 hour in length.

Do your own google searches on floating or floatation therapy to find your own resources. It is getting more popular every day.

The majority of the photos used in this journal came from Vecteezy.com and require no attribution.

Floatosophy is a living document and will continue to evolve as we learn more and more about float therapy. If you have any suggestions for how to improve this tool, we would love to hear your feedback. If you would like to contribute, art, poetry, favorite quotes, or something we have not imagined yet, please let us know by emailing **floatosophy@gmail.com.**

CPSIA information can be obtained
at www.ICGtesting.com
Printed in the USA
BVHW020501030220
571226BV00002B/5